Lucky Socks

Claire Daniel
Illustrated by Bob Dacey

Rigby®
A Harcourt Achieve Imprint

www.Rigby.com
1-800-531-5015

Characters

 Hugo

 Diana, Hugo's older sister

 Mom

 Dad

Scene 1

Narrator: Diana and Hugo are in Diana's room talking about Hugo's first soccer game.

Diana: Are you ready for your first game? Do you have your socks and soccer shoes?

Hugo: I'm ready, but I'm nervous.

Diana: You're going to be great!

Hugo: It's easy for you because you're the star of your team, aren't you?

Diana: No, there are a lot of good players on my team.

Narrator: Hugo watched Diana put a pair of socks on her bed while they talked.

Hugo: Don't you have a pair of lucky socks?

Diana: Yeah, I wore them when I played my first great game, and I've worn them at every game since then.

Hugo: Could I wear them today to help me play a good game?

Narrator: Hugo thought the socks on the bed were Diana's lucky socks.

Diana: My socks are just socks, not anything special.

Hugo: Please let me wear your lucky socks.

Diana: You need to get your own lucky socks.

Hugo: How do I do that?

Diana: You'll learn!

Narrator: Suddenly Diana remembered that she and Hugo needed their water bottles, and she went to get them.

Hugo: She'll never know if I switch the socks.

Narrator: Hugo put the socks from the bed into his bag, and he put the socks from his bag onto the bed.

Narrator: Diana came back carrying two water bottles and a pair of socks.

Diana: We need these!

Narrator: Hugo looked down to put his water bottle into his bag. He didn't notice Diana putting on the pair of socks she had been carrying.

Diana: Let's go!

Scene 2

Narrator: Later that day, the family sat at the dinner table, talking about the soccer games. Hugo had scored the winning goal for his team. Diana had missed a goal, and her team lost.

Mom: You played a great game, Hugo!

Dad: I'm proud of you!

Mom: It's too bad that your team lost, Diana.

Diana: You can't win them all, but I'm mad that I missed the last goal.

Mom: Why are you so quiet, Hugo? You made the winning goal for your team!

Hugo: I didn't do it by myself. Diana, your lucky socks really won the game. I took them from your bed, and I'm sorry. You missed that last goal because I had taken your lucky socks.

Narrator: Diana began to laugh because she had been wearing her lucky socks all day, but her team still hadn't won.

Dad: Don't laugh, Diana. Hugo should never take your things without asking.

Diana: Hugo didn't have my lucky socks because I had them! Hugo took a plain pair of socks, and he must have made them lucky.

Hugo: What do you mean?

Diana: You played well with a pair of plain socks, and now they're lucky socks!

Hugo: You mean I've made my own lucky socks and I can make more lucky socks every time I play well?

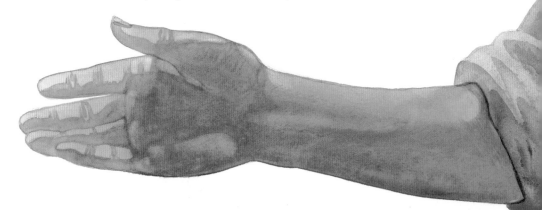

Diana: That sounds like a plan to me!

Hugo: Oh, big sister, you can borrow my lucky socks anytime you want, because I can always get more.